20

18 JU

IL

D1579847

1 3 NOV 2014

2016

OXFORD
UNIVERSITY PRESS

LM 1382519 4

S

OXFORD
UNIVERSITY PRESS

Great Clarendon Street, Oxford OX2 6DP

Oxford University Press is a department of the University of Oxford.
It furthers the University's objective of excellence in research, scholarship,
and education by publishing worldwide in

Oxford   New York

Auckland   Cape Town   Dar es Salaam   Hong Kong   Karachi
Kuala Lumpur   Madrid   Melbourne   Mexico City   Nairobi
New Delhi   Shanghai   Taipei   Toronto

With offices in

Argentina   Austria   Brazil   Chile   Czech Republic   France   Greece
Guatemala   Hungary   Italy   Japan   Poland   Portugal   Singapore
South Korea   Switzerland   Thailand   Turkey   Ukraine   Vietnam

Oxford is a registered trade mark of Oxford University Press
in the UK and in certain other countries

Text © Pippa Goodhart 1996

The moral rights of the author have been asserted

Database right Oxford University Press (maker)

First published 1996
This edition 2005

British Library Cataloguing in Publication Data
Data available

ISBN: 978-0-19-917996-1

17 19 20 18

Available in packs
Stage 12 Pack of 6:
ISBN: 978-0-19-917993-0
Stage 12 Class Pack:
ISBN: 978-0-19-919968-6
Guided Reading Cards also available:
ISBN: 978-0-19-919970-9

Cover artwork by Caroline Holden
Photograph of Pippa Goodhart © Mouse

Printed in Malaysia by
MunSang Printers Sdn Bhd

Paper used in the production of this book is a natural, recyclable product
made from wood grown in sustainable forests. The manufacturing process
conforms to the environmental regulations of the country of origin.

Chapter 1

Sam and Clare were staying for a couple of days with Gran and Grandad. Sam's hamster had come too. Sam put the hamster's cage on the table in the kitchen.

'What's your hamster called, dear?' asked Gran.

'He's called Hamper,' said Sam. 'I called him that because he can carry food around in his cheeks. He can stop and picnic on it wherever he is.'

Hamper was a tiny Russian hamster, hardly bigger than a cotton wool ball.

Grandad put on his glasses and frowned at Hamper's cage from across the room.

'Why do you want a mousy thing like that for a pet?' he asked.

'Because he's nice,' said Sam.

Hamper looked up at Sam with shiny blackcurrant eyes.

'He doesn't like this little cage,' said Sam. 'At home Mum lets him run around the room sometimes. Can I let him out if I watch him? I won't let him run away.'

Gran opened her mouth to reply, but Grandad beat her to it.

'What an idea! Of course you can't let it out.'

'Why not?' asked Sam.

'Because,' said Grandad waggling a finger, 'because if you let that thing loose you'll frighten the life out of your poor Gran. You don't want to do that, do you?'

'No,' said Sam.

'Are *you* scared of any animals, Grandad?' asked Clare. 'When I was little and we went to the zoo, the tigers scared me a bit. They were so big and one of them looked at me and licked his lips.'

7

'Frightened of tigers, eh?' laughed
Grandad. 'When I was a young
fireman I once had to catch a tiger!'

'Really?' said Clare.

'Yes, really,' answered Grandad. 'Of
course we often had to rescue ordinary
cats like Kit-Kat when they got stuck
up trees. But this time the cat up the
tree was a tiger.'

'Really?' asked Clare.

'I put a bowl of smelly fish at the bottom of the tree and that made the tiger climb down. Then I had to get a rope around the tiger's neck!'

'Really?' asked Clare.

'Really,' said Gran, 'but only after the vet had given the tiger an injection to make it sleep.'

'Oh,' said Clare. 'Still, I think you're brave, Grandad.'

Hamper's tiny pink fists held the bars of his cage. He reminded Sam of something he had seen on television. It was about people who were locked up in prison when they hadn't done anything wrong.

'Hamper's cage is like a prison,' he said.

'Well, he's not going to run loose in this house,' said Grandad and he went off into the garden.

10

Sam turned to Clare.

'We don't need to let Hamper out,' he said. 'We can make the cage bigger and more interesting.'

'How?' asked Clare.

'We'll make an extra bit for his cage. A sort of hamster adventure playground.'

Chapter 2

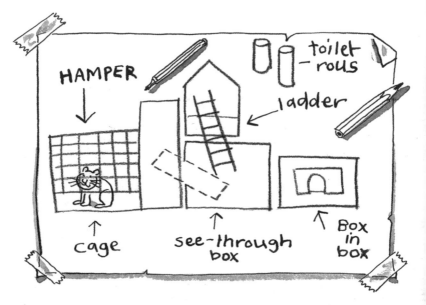

Clare found boxes and loo rolls and cardboard and sticky tape. Sam drew a plan for the adventure playground.

'It's going to twist up and down and round,' he said. 'Use that see-through box, Clare. Then we can watch Hamper.'

'Don't boss me!' said Clare.

There was one long cardboard tube.
'That can be a slide,' said Clare.

There was a margarine tub that Sam
filled with dried peas and put at the
bottom of the slide.

'A hamster ball pool,' he said.

They stuck more and more bits and pieces together. Soon the playground was twice the size of Hamper's cage.

'It looks good, doesn't it?' said Sam. 'I wish I could shrink and have a go in it with Hamper.'

Lunch was almost ready and Grandad came in from the garden.

'What are we having for lunch?' he asked.

'Fish fingers,' said Gran.

'Come and see Hamper's adventure playground, Grandad,' said Sam.

'Adventure playground, eh?' said Grandad. 'I once had to rescue a fish from a fairground.'

'Really?' said Clare.

'Yup,' said Grandad. 'The fish got its fingers stuck in the big wheel. The fingers came right off. Your Gran put them in the freezer and now we've got them for lunch.'

'Oh, Grandad!' laughed Clare. 'I don't believe that one.'

16

'I did once save a fish, though,' said Grandad. 'A family's house was on fire. We got the mother and father and two little girls out, but one of the girls was crying for her goldfish. I went back through the smoke and flames to get him out, too. It's not easy carrying a goldfish bowl down a ladder.'

'It was brave to go back into the fire,' said Clare. 'Weren't you scared?'

'Oh, I was scared all right,' said Grandad. 'Being brave doesn't mean that you aren't scared. Being brave means that you do something even though it scares you.'

'Oh!' said Clare.

Sam had a problem. 'How can I open Hamper's door after I've fixed the playground to the cage? Can you help please, Grandad?'

'I can,' said Gran. 'What you need to do is tie a bit of string to the cage door. Then pull it through a small hole in the cardboard. Now you can open the door without Hamper escaping.'

'Brilliant!' said Sam. 'How did you think of that?'

'Oh, I was like you when I was your age,' said Gran. 'I made things for my animals too.'

'What sort of animals did you have?' asked Sam. But Gran didn't answer him.

'Let Hamper into his playground now. He can play there while we have lunch,' she said. 'Then you two go and wash your hands.'

I'll ask her about her pets later, thought Sam.

Sam pushed the door string through a hole in the cardboard. Then he fixed the playground to Hamper's cage.

'O.K.,' said Sam. 'Here goes. Five, four, three, two, one!'

He pulled on the string and the door opened. Hamper pulled himself up and over into the playground. There was a scratchy, slithery noise as he zoomed down the first slide and into the ball pool.

'Look!' said Clare. She pointed to
the see-through box where Hamper
was sitting, tail down, in the dried
peas. 'He likes it!'

'Of course he does,' said Sam.

Chapter 3

The noises from Hamper's cage and playground stopped during lunch. Perhaps Hamper had got tired, thought Sam. Perhaps he was having a rest.

When lunch was finished, Gran and Grandad went to have a cup of tea. Sam went to look for Hamper.

He couldn't see Hamper in the cage. Sam listened at each part of the playground in turn but there were no hamster noises.

'Clare!' said Sam, 'I can't find Hamper!'

'He must be there somewhere!' said Clare. 'I bet he's asleep in one of the tubes.'

'We'll have to check,' said Sam. 'Quick, before Gran comes in.'

He gently pulled one tube out of the playground and peered down it.

'I can't see anything,' he said.

'Blow down it,' said Clare.

Sam blew. He blew as hard as he could, but no small fluffy hamster came out of the bottom of the tube.

He pulled more parts of the playground to bits.

'After you made me stick them all together!' said Clare.

'We've got to find him,' said Sam.

He worked faster and faster, pulling apart all the tubes and boxes until the playground was just a pile of rubbish on the floor. Then Sam held up one of the boxes. It had a hole the size of a fifty pence piece chewed through one corner.

'He's got out!' said Sam.

'Oh, no!' said Clare. 'What about Gran? If she sees Hamper it'll scare the life out of her.'

'And if Kit-Kat sees Hamper, Kit-Kat will scare the life out of *him!*' said Sam. 'We've got to find him fast.'

Sam stood up.

'Look!' he said. 'Hamster sneezes!'

The pepper pot on Gran's worktop had been knocked over and spilt. There were tiny hamster footprints across the fine brown pepper powder. Two small triangles had been sneezed from a little hamster nose.

'Bless him!' said Sam.

At least they had a clue.

'He went that way.' Clare pointed in the direction the footprints were heading.

'Oh, look!'

There were more footprints, red ones. Hamper had gone across the dirty plates left from lunch. He had put one paw into some tomato ketchup. Now there were tiny red footprints across to the edge of the worktop and a red streak down the cupboard door.

'He's down on the floor somewhere,' said Sam.

30

Chapter 4

Sam and Clare both got down on hands and knees. They put their heads down and peered under tables, chairs, and cupboards.

'Oh no, watch out!' whispered Sam. He had seen Gran's fluffy slippers coming through the door.

'What are you two doing down there?' asked Gran.

Clare jumped up. 'We've lost –'
'A button!' said Sam. 'We've lost a
button and we think it's on the floor.'

Then Sam saw something else
coming through the door. Four ginger
paws with claws. It was Kit-Kat!

Kit-Kat walked into the kitchen and stopped. He stuck his nose in the air and sniffed. Then, with his tail up, Kit-Kat walked slowly across the floor to the place where a radiator pipe went into the floor.

The hole that the pipe went through was bigger than the pipe. Sam could see that there was just enough room around it for a small hamster to squeeze through.

Sam looked at Clare. Clare looked at Sam.

'Er, we'll do the washing up, Gran,' said Clare. 'You go and sit down or something!'

'Are you sure?' asked Gran, but Sam was already pushing her through the kitchen door and Clare was picking up Kit-Kat and pushing him out too. Sam closed the door.

They stood and looked at the hole where Hamper had gone. Suddenly a small nose appeared.

'There he is!' said Sam. 'Quick, get his food, Clare! Come on, Hampy.'

The nose didn't move.

'Try a sunflower seed,' said Sam.

'You're not the boss!' said Clare. But she held a sunflower seed between a finger and thumb.

The nose came a bit further out.

'Good boy!' said Clare and she let Hamper take the seed.

'I can't get hold of him,' said Sam. 'His nose is too small to hold on to.'

'All right,' said Clare. 'That one was just to give him the idea.'

She offered Hamper another seed.

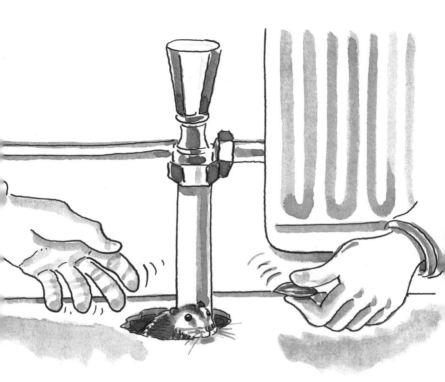

This time his nose and eyes came out
of the hole before she let him eat it.

'He's got to be more out than that,'
said Sam.

'I know!' said Clare.

Next time the nose, the eyes, and the
ears came out.

'He's getting better!' said Clare.

'Hurry up!' said Sam, glancing at the
door.

Clare held out another seed. Out came the nose, eyes, and ears. She moved the seed further back.

'Come right out!' she said and Hamper did try to come right out, but –

'Oh, no!' said Sam. 'He can't fit. We've filled his cheeks up with seeds and now he can't fit through. He's stuck!'

'Oh dear,' said Clare. 'What shall we do?'

'We'll have to tell Grandad,' said Sam.

Chapter 5

Sam went and got Grandad and brought him into the kitchen.

'What's this all about?' asked Grandad. 'What's so secret?'

'Hamper's escaped,' whispered Clare, 'and we don't want Gran to know in case it scares the life out of her!'

'Escaped?' said Grandad. His voice was strangely high-up. 'Where? Where is it?'

'He's under the floor,' said Clare.

'No, he's not!' said Sam. 'He's come out. Look!'

There was Hamper sitting on the kitchen floor. And a moment later there was Grandad standing on a chair.

'Grandad?' said Sam. 'What are you doing?'

'Take it away!' whispered Grandad.
'Just get that mousy thing out of here!'

Sam picked Hamper up.

'Don't be scared,' said Sam. 'He's
only tiny.'

Clare patted Grandad's leg.
'Grandad is scared, but he's brave too,'
she said. 'Grandad's so brave that he
does things even when he *is* scared,
don't you, Grandad?'

41

'Will he hold Hamper, then?' asked Sam.

Grandad nodded slowly, then he climbed down from the chair. He held out his large knobbly hands. Very gently, Sam tipped tiny brown Hamper into them.

For a moment nobody moved. Then Grandad laughed a small laugh. He stroked Hamper's soft warm head and back with one big finger.

'Hello, little fellow,' said Grandad.

Hamper looked at Grandad with his shiny blackcurrant eyes.

Grandad laughed again.

'You know I never thought I would say this, but you are right, Sam. This little mousy thing is rather nice!'

Gran stood in the doorway.

'Well I'm blessed!' she said. 'After all these years.'

'Aren't you frightened of him, Gran?' said Clare.

'No,' laughed Gran. 'I've always loved mice and hamsters. I used to keep rats when I was a girl. It's your Grandad who's scared of them. Ever since he was a boy.'

'Why?' asked Sam.

'Well,' said Grandad, cradling little Hamper between his two hands. 'It was when I was about your age, Sam.'

45

Grandad went on, 'My friend Tony and I spent a night in his father's barn. We laid blankets over the sweet new hay. You couldn't have asked for a more comfortable bed. But in the dark, dark middle of the night I woke up. A mouse ran across my face! Can you imagine that?

'I sat up, scared stiff. I couldn't see a thing. For the whole of the rest of the night I sat listening to the scratching and squeaking all around me. I've never liked mice since that night.'

46

'Until now,' said Sam.

Hamper suddenly ran up Grandad's arm. Grandad went pale and stiff. Then Hamper tickled under Grandad's chin and Grandad laughed.

'Until now, I suppose,' he said.

About the author

When I was a child I longed
to have lots of animals.
I once brought the
school hamster home for
a weekend. The hamster
ran away through a hole
in the wall and then filled
his cheeks so full of food
that he couldn't fit back.

Remembering that started me off on
this story about Hamper. Nowadays I live
with my husband and three little daughters
who all need feeding and cleaning and
grooming so I don't long for animals as much
as I once did. Still, we do have a big hairy dog
and a naughty kitten.